THE LITTLE BOOK ABOUT
NUMBERS FOR PEOPLE WHO
WOULD REALLY RATHER NOT
HAVE TO READ ABOUT NUMBERS

THE LITTLE BOOK ABOUT NUMBERS FOR PEOPLE WHO WOULD REALLY RATHER NOT HAVE TO READ ABOUT NUMBERS

DR YVONNE TOMMIS

All rights reserved

© 2018 by Yvonne Tommis

The right of Yvonne Tommis to be identified as author of this work has been asserted in accordance with Section 77 of the Copyright, Designs and Patents Act 1988. This book or any portion thereof may not be reproduced or used in any manner whatsoever without the express written permission of the publisher except for the use of brief quotations in a book review or scholarly journal.

First printing: 2018

ISBN: 978-0-9556848-4-5

Published by Seriol House: seriolhouse@gmail.com

Contents

Introduction i

Acknowledgements iii

CHAPTER ONE 1
    THE HUMBLE PERCENTAGE 1
    A tale of two pigs *1*

CHAPTER TWO 12
    THE NOT SO HUMBLE PERCENTAGE AND MONEY 12

CHAPTER THREE 23
    AVERAGES 23
    The meaningless nature of the mean *23*

CHAPTER FOUR 33
    CORRELATION 33
    A cautionary revision tale *33*

CHAPTER FIVE 38
    STANDARD DEVIATION 38
    A tale of two donkeys *38*

CHAPTER SIX 47
    CONFIDENCE INTERVALS 47
    The unConfident Cat *47*

CHAPTER SEVEN 53

THE CHI-SQUARE..53

and the Pig Whisperer..*53*

CHAPTER EIGHT 68

THE *T* TEST 68

And finally...81

Introduction

Numbers are nice – no, really, they are nice! Numbers are lovely. Unfortunately many people have had bad experiences with numbers and so approach them with apprehension. Furthermore there can also be an element of mistrust, it can often seem that people are just plucking figures out of thin air in order to justify their argument. This mistrust is understandable as people will use numbers to deceive, they will manipulate them to support their argument, and some people will be quite unscrupulous in the way they do so.

But isn't that what people do with words? Misconstrue, misquote and other mis-manipulations? You may feel reasonably confident in dealing with that though; confident you can spot when it's happening. You probably feel less confident that you can spot when it is happening with numbers, the very sight of which can induce something akin to mild panic (or even not so mild panic depending on the context).

So this little book has two big aims:
- To help you become confident in reading material that uses numbers. So that rather than experiencing the eyes glazing over panicky feeling, you feel able to read slowly and understand what is being said. Once you understand what is being said you will then be able to also make a judgment about its accuracy. Can they really claim what they are

claiming? Are numbers being used to distort and deceive? Or perhaps to exaggerate?

- The second aim is to provide you with skills to use numbers in your everyday life and perhaps to also use numbers appropriately in your own work.

Perhaps you're a student and have been dreading a module that you know will mean you have to look at some numbers, well, this little book is here to help!

This book will not explain how to conduct complicated statistical procedures such multivariate regression analysis. Or any regression analysis at all in fact. Or to conduct an ANOVA or any of the other complicated statistical procedures you may have heard people talking about. And if you have never heard of any of those things, then that is absolutely fine too and you are going to feel at home with this book. This book really is going to keep things simple. If after reading it you're so inspired that you want to learn how to do the more complicated things, there are lots of people out there to help you. For now we're just going to stick with the basic stuff, and remember, numbers are nice!

You do not have to start at the beginning and work your way through to the end, although the book is structured so that the more straightforward topics occur early on and the more complicated ones towards the end. However, each of the chapters is focused on an individual topic so if something you really want to know about is in the middle, start there.

Acknowledgements

There are many people whose help has been invaluable in putting this little book together and I would like to say a big thank you to them all. I would like to thank Professor Lynn Hodgkinson for her early encouragement to continue with the book, and not leave it in a folder in the depths of my computer. She also read many of the chapters and both suggested improvements and noticed typos that had escaped my attention (0.42 instead of .042, not a good one to make!) I would like to thank Katie Evans, who despite not being a numbers person valiantly read through the early chapters and provided very useful feedback. And also thank you to Dr Jo Wells, who was very good at noticing the risk of confusion.

A couple of computer programs are mentioned, but there are many others. Further information on the ones mentioned can be found at:

For Microsoft Excel: https://products.office.com/en-gb/excel

For SPSS: http://www.ibm.com/analytics/us/en/technology/spss/

CHAPTER ONE

The Humble Percentage

A tale of two pigs

Betsy sighed and leant against the wall of her sty "I really wish I could win that holiday for a Week in Paradise" she said wistfully as she lowered her copy of Destinations for the Discerning Traveller. Elizabeth put down her copy of Oink! magazine and sighed too as she heard that comment at least three times a day.

"It's not really paradise you know," she replied "that's just what they call the holiday."

"I know that, it just sounds so good. They make a list of all your favourite things and then surprise you with them when you're there."

"Not really a surprise if you've already......" Elizabeth's reply was interrupted as she tried to dodge the magazine that was being thrown in her direction. As it flew through the air a small piece of paper fell from it into Betsy's sty who picked it up and read it intently.

"Elizabeth, this is amazing! I know how to win the holiday! It says here! It says that pigs who eat from the Lucky Trough are 50% more likely to win the holiday than those who don't! Where is that trough? I need to eat from it now!"

"Calm down Betsy, you'll have a heart attack and miss the holiday." Betsy glared at Elizabeth.

1

"Killjoy! You are so boring!"

"No I'm not, I'd really like you to win the holiday but that 50% is practically meaningless."

"Why? 50% is a lot!"

"No, 50% **can** be a lot but it can also be a very little."

"But it's 50%, it has to be a lot!"

"It's 50% of what exactly?"

Betsy picked up the piece of paper again "It says here that 50% more pigs who eat from the lucky trough win the holiday than ordinary pigs. See....."

"Ok" interrupted Elizabeth, "So how many pigs actually win the competition. See if you can find out how many pigs who enter the competition without eating from the lucky trough win the holiday."

Betsy was silent for awhile as she googled the competition on her iPad.

"Got it!" she finally said, and then sounded quite despondent "out of every hundred thousand pigs who enter only one will win the holiday. That's not very many is it?"

"No it isn't." agreed Elizabeth. "So if 50% more pigs who eat from the lucky trough win, how many will win the holiday?"

Betsy screwed up her snout "Well 50% of one is a half. So 50% more pigs would be one and a half pigs. But you can't have half a pig!"

"So it would be two pigs out of two hundred thousand who normally win the holiday, and three pigs out of two hundred thousand who eat from the lucky trough."

"Seems to me that the trough isn't so lucky after all. But I don't get it, 50% sounds like it's a lot."

"You need to remember that a percentage is always a percentage of something. So if you only have a very small amount in the first place, even an increase of 50% will be tiny."

"Sneaky blobberdigoats!" exclaimed Betsy. "That's why the leaflet was there! They want to charge pigs to eat from the lucky trough! That's why they're saying 50% more likely! If they said one and a half pigs per hundred thousand win compared to one pig per hundred thousand no one would take them up on the offer."

"Got it in one," agreed Elizabeth as she turned over to go to sleep.

Like Betsy, we all understand percentages. We know that 100% means everyone, 50% half the people, and 2% almost no-one. However, the major problem with a percentage is that it has to be a percentage of something, and it's that 'something' that can cause the problems. It's because of this that percentages can be used very easily to present a misleading picture, and they frequently are. Sometimes this is maybe intentional, as in the lucky trough example, but more frequently it is the result of the writer stating a fact (an 'increase of 25%', or '50% more likely', for example) and the reader assuming that it must be a lot simply because of the percentage figure. So in this chapter we'll look at some examples, but before we do a quick refresher: what is a percentage?

A percentage is a way of representing things so that they can be easily compared. We can say that 23 out of 54 males are scared of spiders and 54 out of 80 females, but it's not immediately obvious whether more females than males are scared of spiders. The most we can easily see from the figures is that under half of males are (half of 54 would be 27), while over half of females are (half of 80 would be 40), but that's as far as we can go. Calculating both as a percentage means we can directly compare them in a more meaningful way.

To work out the number of males who are scared of spiders as a percentage:

> Divide the number of males who are scared of spiders by the total number of males, which is:
>
> $23 \div 54 = 0.425925$
>
> then multiply 0.425925 by 100 to give the percentage
>
> $= 42.59\%$
>
> So, 43% of males are scared of spiders.

The same calculation for females is:

> Divide the number of females who are scared of spiders by the total number of females, which is:
>
> $54 \div 80 = 0.675$
>
> then multiply 0.675×100 to give the percentage
>
> $= 67.5\%$
>
> So, 68% of females are afraid of spiders.

We can now see that quite a few more females than males are scared of spiders.

Moving away from spiders to believing in life after death. (Well it wasn't even worth attempting to link the two.) Here's an imaginary headline from an imaginary newspaper:

"British Social Attitudes Survey shows that 35% believe in life after death!"

Your first reaction may be that 35% sounds rather more people than would be expected. Our imaginary journalist took their figures from the Wales data of the British Social Attitudes Survey, 2008, which is a real dataset. The survey covers a number of topics, including whether the respondent believes in life after death.

Here's the relevant table:

	N	% of all	% of valid
Absolutely sure do believe	19	8.8%	16.4%
Somewhat sure do believe	22	10.2%	19.0%
Not quite sure	23	10.7%	19.8%
Not at all sure	20	9.3%	17.2%
Sure do not believe	32	14.9%	27.6%
No answer	99	46.0%	
TOTAL	215	100.0%	100.0%

When first looking at a table do not panic – remember to read slowly!

The column on the far left represents the reply options the respondent had to choose from. The question was *'Do you believe in life after death?'* Available responses ranged from *'Absolutely sure do believe'* through to *'Sure do not believe'*. Also notice that 'No answer' is included to record the number of people who simply left all options blank. Sometimes a survey will give the respondent the opportunity to not answer the question by including a *'Don't know'* or *'Rather not say'* reply option. That was not the case with this question. The final row provides the totals for each of the columns.

The next column is 'n', or sometimes labelled 'frequency'. This is the number of people who responded in that category. So 19 people indicated that they were *'Absolutely sure do believe'*; 22 that they were *'Somewhat sure do believe'*; 23 *'Not quite sure'* etc.. The very bottom figure tells us that 215 people participated in the survey (from Wales).

The '% of all' column gives the percentage of people responding in the category as a percentage of the total number of people participating. Remember that 19 people responded *'Absolutely sure do believe'*. To work out the percentage this is of all people:

19 divided by 215 (the total number of people) = 0.088

0.088 multiplied by 100 (to get the percentage) = **8.8%**.

This percentage includes people who did not answer the question at all. That is really important. The % of all is exactly what it says, it is a percentage of everyone from Wales who participated in the survey, even if they did not answer the question we are looking at.

The final column '% of valid' only takes into consideration the people who answered the question. Only 116 answered the question: [215 (total) − 99 (who did not answer the question) = 116] so to calculate this valid percentage for the 19 people who responded *'Absolutely sure do believe'*:

19÷116 (the number of people who answered the question)
= 0.164
0.164 ×100 = **16.4%**.

This is the percentage of people who answered the question and stated *'Absolutely sure do believe'*.

Quite a difference! Just taking one response category, *'Absolutely sure do believe'*, we can either say that 8.8% or 16.4% of people fall into that category! Which figure we chose could well be influenced by the picture we wanted to paint.

Quite often different answer categories are combined to give fewer categories. So in this example we could combine *'Absolutely sure do believe'* with *'Somewhat sure do believe'* to give an overall *'Believe'* category. There are 19 + 22 = 41 people in this new category. Calculating percentages for this category:

Percentage of all = 41÷215 = 0.191

0.191 × 100 = **19.1%**.

Therefore, 19% of **all** respondents believe in life after death.

For only those who answered the question:

Valid percent = 41÷116 = 0.3534

0.3534 × 100 = **35.34%**.

So 35% of respondents who **answered the question** believe in life after death. That sentence is too long for a headline though, so it's easier (if mis-leading) to shorten it to "35% believe in life after death".

Does that figure really represent people's beliefs? No, not at all. The problem is the 99 people who did not answer the question. That is a lot of people, in fact it's 46% of the people who took part (in Wales). Or, put another way, almost half of the people who completed the survey did not answer the question relating to life after death beliefs. What that effectively means is that the responses to the question are virtually useless. We may be tempted to say that almost half of all respondents were reluctant to answer the question – but we cannot even say that! We do not know why they did not answer it, perhaps it was near the end and they simply couldn't be bothered to answer any more questions, we do not know. If there had been an answer option of *'Prefer not to answer'* and 99 people had chosen that response then we could say that 46%

of people preferred not to answer a question relating to belief in life and death; but there wasn't so we can't.

So how can we spot these percentage misquotes? By remembering that a percentage has to be a percentage **of** something. If a headline read "41 people believe in life after death" we would ignore it and be rather confused as to why it was there in the first place. We would probably also look further down the page (assuming we could be bothered) to try and find out where these 41 people came from. The "35% believe in life after death" is in the same category; 35% of what? If the article we're reading doesn't tell us the 'of what' then we need to find the source data before being able to use the figure. If we cannot find the source data then we simply cannot use it – it is meaningless.

Unfortunately organisations we may normally think of as being trustworthy are not immune to this:

A few years ago a BBC News Report[1] stated that being obese in middle age increased the likelihood of suffering from dementia by 74%. This alarming percentage was presented in the television news reports with no other figures, while the website article did contain more information for those with the patience to read on. The web article began with "Obese people in their 40s are 74%

---

[1] http://news.bbc.co.uk/1/hi/health/4492745.stm

more likely to develop dementia compared to those of normal weight, a US National Institute of Health team found". That is a good way of getting someone's attention! Hopefully, after reading the tale of two pigs you are now wondering what the likelihood of developing dementia in the non-obese population is; what is the 74% increase an increase of? The article does not give that figure, but it does state "Overall, 713 (7%) of the participants developed dementia." The study followed 10,000 people, and of those 713 developed dementia. Breaking the figures down gives:

For 10,000 people, the number of non-obese people developing dementia would be 412 = 4.12% (the study did not actually quote those figures, they're obtained through a backwards calculation). For obese people the figure rises to 713 (7.13%).

There is no doubt that according to the US study being obese does increase the risk of developing dementia, a rise from 4% to 7%. However, a headline stating that being obese increases the risk of dementia from 4% to 7% is not very attention grabbing, whereas one stating that being obese in middle age increases the risk of developing dementia by 74% is. Is the headline inaccurate? No. Is it mis-leading? Probably, but not anymore. Buried in the article is a statement that the lifetime dementia risk was 35% higher. By focussing on people in their 40's the headline is much more dramatic. A further complication is that it may not be the obesity itself that is causing an increased risk of dementia, it could easily be another factor commonly found alongside obesity. A study would have to look at all contributing factors and conduct an appropriate (and complicated) analysis before being able to state with any certainty that obesity itself was the link. A well thought out research study will have included this in its findings, but unfortunately it is not the case that all will do so. In general, caution needs to be exercised when looking at this kind of 'standing on one leg for an hour a day decreases the risk of heart attack' headline. People are very complicated and rarely is a single thing the cause of something else, and it can take years of research to prove a definitive link, think of how long it took with smoking and lung cancer.

CHAPTER TWO

The Not So Humble Percentage and Money

Betsy was staring at her iPad with a frown on her face. Elizabeth looked across and saw the frown turn to a broad smile as Betsy clapped her trotters with glee, "I can do it after all" she said "I can go on the weekend luxury spa break!"

"I thought you didn't have enough money for that," commented Elizabeth. "Have you found some hiding somewhere?"

"No, no, but I've found this website that offers something called a Payday Loan and it looks really good! It's two weeks until we get paid so I can borrow £200 from them now and then pay back £233 when I get paid – brilliant!"

"Betsy, that really does not sound very good at all."

"Why? It's only an extra £33, that's not much!"

"But it's a huge interest rate! What if you can't repay it in 2 weeks time?"

"But we always get paid on the last day of the month!"

"Normally we do yes, but just humour me on this one. Imagine our human has a heart attack and dies or something."

"Oh I don't want to think of that, he's so kind. He gave me a cup cake last week!" Elizabeth sighed but decided she had to persevere.

"I know it's not nice to think about it. But if you didn't get paid then you wouldn't be able to pay them back so what would happen?"

It was Betsy's turn to sigh as she looked at her iPad, "I don't know. Can't seem to find out. Maybe I'd have to take out another loan to pay off the first one?"

"Why don't we work out the interest rate; that would be useful. You have to pay back £33 on £200?"

"Yes, that's right. Oh there's a £5 admin charge so the interest is only £28!" Elizabeth took her calculator down from the wall and began to push some buttons.

"Ok" said Elizabeth as she made herself comfortable on some straw "28 divided by 200..."

"Hang on a minute!" interrupted Betsy "What exactly are you doing?"

"I'm working out the interest rate. We take the extra amount that you have to pay, which is £28, and divide it by the amount you borrow, which is £200, then multiply that by 100 to make it a percentage. So 28 divided by 200 is 0.14, multiply by 100 gives 14. The interest rate is 14%."

"That's not too bad!" Betsy was sounding excited again.

"Hang on hang on, patience and virtues etc.. That's 14% over 14 days which is 1% a day. So if you kept the money for a year the interest rate would be 365%!"

Betsy was beginning to look worried. "And I thought credit cards were bad at 20% interest. I'm going to look again to see what happens if I can't pay it back on time."

Betsy was silent for quite a few minutes as she delved further into the website. Eventually she sighed and said "I'd be really stuck if the money wasn't there. They automatically take the payment from my account and charge £20 if it's not there. Then there's all sorts of scary stuff about phoning me and if I haven't repaid it within 60 days it goes to a debt collection agency. I don't like that at all!"

"So is it worth the risk just to go on a luxury spa weekend?"

"No, maybe my great grandmother was right after all; better to save up for something like a luxury spa weekend. I'll get one of those really cute little Human Banks and start saving. Money is just so complicated and difficult, I'm really glad I'm not human!"

It was a few days later when Elizabeth saw Betsy standing in the corner of her sty looking quite forlorn. "Betsy, what's wrong?" she asked.

"Oh, nothing really, I've just been talking to our human that's all." Elizabeth was quite concerned at this "He didn't upset you did he?"

"No, not at all. I'm just surprised that I knew more about mortgage stuff than he did! Do you remember when I was thinking of taking out that Payday loan? Well, after that I decided I needed to know more about borrowing money and interest rates so I found some good websites and learnt about APR etc.. That took me some time to get my head around! But I now know that APR stands for Annual Percentage Rate and it's supposed to make comparing the cost of different loans easier. Turns out our human is looking for a new mortgage but he's getting confused by the different fees involved and the differences between an initial interest rate and the APR. He was trying to compare just by taking the option with the lowest APR rate and couldn't understand why that didn't have the lowest monthly payments."

"Betsy, I am seriously impressed that you've worked so hard on this!"

"I'm actually quite impressed with myself! So I explained to him that basically he couldn't take any short cuts and that he had to look at any fees that were charged, and decide whether he wanted to take out a fixed term interest rate for a number of years and then change mortgages again after that. It really is very complicated though."
"It is indeed. Do you think you convinced him?"
"Yes definitely. He had thought he could just compare the APR, but he knows now that he can't. He did tell me something amusing though."
"Do tell."
"I was saying how my great grandmother was very good with money and he said that when she was younger she got out one day and ran all the way to Edinburgh!"
"Edinburgh! That's miles away! Why did she go there?"
"Turns out the Royal Family were visiting so as they were doing a walkabout on Princes Street she ran down the middle of the road waving a flag that said 'If you love animals don't eat them'! Can you imagine any pig doing that!"
"Oh, I can imagine your great grandmother doing lots of things."
"Pigs say I'm quite like her, but I don't think I am."
"But" said Elizabeth as she lay down on her most comfortable spot "do any of us know how we appear to be to others." When the expected reply didn't materialise she turned and looked across to Betsy, who was already fast asleep.

Percentages and money can be the most difficult and confusing percentages to understand, which is a pity because they are also extremely important. There are no short cuts with this, it really is a case of making sure you understand whatever it is that you're looking at. Regulations state that companies must provide the APR (Annual Percentage Rate) of any loan they are offering. This can be very helpful if you're looking to borrow money for 3 years to buy a car, where it can fall down is with something like a mortgage. Even with a straightforward loan there are actually two different APR's, there's the 'Representative APR' and the 'Personal APR'. The Representative APR is the one that they must provide to a certain percentage of customers and use in advertising, however, they do not have to provide it to everyone! There is no guarantee that if you take out the loan you will actually be charged the Representative APR. Companies can vary the rate according to a person's credit rating and so may charge a higher interest rate to some people. They will have to state this interest rate as the 'Personal APR', so that must be checked to make sure that it is OK. Confusing – yes!

Mortgages are usually taken out over a long period of time and so can have different problems. Imagine you're taking out a mortgage for 10 years. Many companies have a cheaper fixed rate option where the interest rate is lower for the first few years (usually between 2 and 5) of the mortgage, before reverting back to the 'standard variable rate' for the remainder of the time. The initial monthly payments will be lower during this fixed rate period, which can make it an appealing option. Many people take out a fixed rate mortgage for a two or three years and then move to another mortgage when the fixed rate period expires. By doing this they manage to avoid paying the Standard Variable Rate (which is usually higher).

The problem is that the APR will have to be calculated over the lifetime of the mortgage, even if your intention is to move your mortgage when the fixed rate ends. So a 2 year fixed rate deal with a lower interest rate could easily have a higher APR than a 4 year fixed rate deal because more of the 10 years will be at the higher, non fixed, rate! The fees that are charged when taking out the loan also need to be taken into consideration. If a two-year fixed rate mortgage has an arrangement fee of £1,500 then that is actually an extra £31.25 a month, so a fee free mortgage that is £25 a month more expensive will be cheaper.

As Elizabeth said, there really are no short cuts, you just have to sit down with a piece of paper and pen (or computer and spreadsheet) and make a note of all the costs involved. Only then can a proper comparison be made. Of course, there will always be an element of luck/guesswork or financial judgement (depending on your point of view). When interest rates are low the percentages quoted for a five year fixed rate will be higher than those quoted for a two or three year fixed rate. This is so that any increase in interest rates can be absorbed into the quoted interest rate. The mortgage company want to avoid a future situation where people are paying substantially less for an existing older fixed rate mortgage than new customers are for their new mortgage. But when you are staring at the piece of paper you have no idea what interest rates will be like in three or four years' time. If they increase you could find yourself pleased that you paid a little extra for the first year or so as you are now paying less. If they stay the same you could find yourself wishing you'd chosen a different option. Unless you can see into the future there is no easy answer to that one. The important thing is to understand what all those percentages and fees actually mean! Follow Betsy's example and take the time to understand what's involved. Remember to read slowly. Whenever money is involved read very slowly, and then read it again even more slowly! Good Luck!

Shopping!
(If you are confident working out percentage discounts then feel free to skip this section)

"Fliggerbigibert and flibberbigibert and oodle noodles!" Betsy was cross, very cross.
"What in the name of my trotters is wrong!" asked Elizabeth as she came back into her sty to see huge trotterfuls of straw flying in all directions, with far too many flying in her direction.
"The coach is leaving in half an hour and I can't find it!" replied Betsy tossing another piece of straw to one side.
"Ah, the shopping trip. So what can't you find? Your ticket? Your debit card?"
"No no no!" interrupted Betsy "I've got all of those, I can't find that piece of paper where you explained how to work out discounted prices. You know the 15% or 20% off ones. I think I'm going to need it as a lot of prices will have discounts!"
"OK, I get it now. But Betsy it's really not too difficult, and you'll have the calculator on your phone."
"Oink oink! Not using that. What kind of pig can be seen working out a discount in a shop! Not this super smart super cool one!"
"No-one would know that was what you're doing. You could just be sending a text, or doing a facebook update on the status of your trip. Betsy stop and sit down and listen. I'll explain it again!"
"How am I going to remember? I think there's going to be some amazing hats there. Can't imagine why you don't want to come too."

"Betsy, stop!" This time Elizabeth spoke in her sternest of don't ignore me voices and Betsy finally stopped tossing straw everywhere and sat down to listen.

"OK shoot. You've got ten minutes."

"First, if you're working out the discount in your head remember that you don't have to work to the nearest penny. A lot of prices are £3.99 or £4.99 or £16.99, so just round the original price up to the nearest pound. So if something's £21.99, work out the discount from £22.00."

"I do remember how to do a 10% discount. Move the decimal point one place to the left and then subtract. So 10% of £22.00 is £2.20 and £22.00 take away £2.20 is £19.80. But how far away from that is the accurate answer?"

"I'll use the calculator on my phone and tell you. "£21.99 take away £2.199 is £19.79. Close enough for you?"

"Definitely! But what if the discount is 15%? How do I work that out?"

"Start off with 10% as before. Now you need to take away another 5%, which is half of 10%, so you need to take away half of £2.20 from our original answer."

"Got it! It'll be £19.80 take away £1.10 which is £18.70?"

"You got it. Or you could say that 10% is £2.20, another 5% is £1.10 so I'll take £3.30 from the original £22.00. 22 take away 3 is 19, and £19 take away 30 pence is £18.70."

"My brain is hurting, there isn't enough space for all those numbers!"

"You just need to practice it that's all. How would you work out a 20% discount?"

"Double the 10%!"

"You could, or you could divide by 5."

"Oink! Just when I thought I was getting the hang of it you have to go and change it. Flibberghosts!"

"It's worth remember that 20% of something is one fifth of it. Also remember that 25% is one quarter, and it's easier to divide by 4 than take away two 10%'s followed by half of a 10%."

"S'pose so. No choice with 30% and 40% is there. Have to multiply 10% by 3 and 4. Even I know that if something is 50% off it's half price. I really hope that I get some of those!"

"If you get something really complicated you'll have to use the calculator on your phone, but there's no need to use the percentage button at all."

"Great as I'm never sure how that works, and I don't think my new phone has one anyway."

"10% is actually 10 divided by 100 which is 0.1. So to find 10% of anything just multiply it by 0.1. For 15% multiply it by 0.15, for 20% by 0.2 etc.. etc.. You can then just take away the original number without having to type everything in again. Gives a negative answer but the number is correct."

"Hang on" said Betsy as she found the calculator on her phone. "So if it is 15% off £22.00 I can do 22 times 0.15, which gives 3.3. Now all I have to do take away 22 and it gives the answer as -18.7. I know it's not really negative and that the answer is actually £18.70. Not bad Elizabeth dearest. I may use that if no-one's watching."

"Or if the price is complicated. I wouldn't like to tackle 15% off £38.75 in my head!"

"Well 15% of £38.75 is £3.875 plus around £1.93 which is £5.80 ish. So it would be £38.75 minus £5.80 which is £32.95."

Elizabeth was so surprised that she fell against the side of her sty, mouth open in amazement. Betsy smiled across at her and winked.

"Surprised? All it takes is a little motivation."

CHAPTER THREE

Averages

The meaningless nature of the mean

The lions were furious. "I am the king of the jungle!" roared one "How dare those cheetah upstarts claim they are worth more! Their average income is definitely not higher than ours!"
Cedric the cheetah cowered behind a tree hoping the ground would stop shaking soon. He was fully aware of the lions' superiority and had absolutely no desire to challenge it. "What are we going to do Jemimah?" he said to his mate, who was cowering behind the same tree.
"Find a bigger tree," responded Jemimah. Cedric flicked his tail at her and showed her the cause of their problems. Someone had put in a freedom of information request to the park rangers and discovered how much the animals earned. Over the last month the lions had earned an average of 738 South African Rand while the average for the cheetahs was just over 42,000 South African Rand. No wonder the lions were cross.
Jemimah sighed as she looked at the figures "I don't want to fight with the lions either, they are bigger than us and stronger than us. I just want to hide. I don't understand where those figures have come from."
Cedric turned the piece of paper over to look at the table showing the earnings for each individual cat:

Lions		Cheetahs	
SK	1000	J	420
L	670	K	380
MJ	810	S	510
D	520	PT	475
EW	680	C	250,000
FW	750	AZ	320
MEAN	738	MEAN	42,018

"It's all my fault!" Cedric exclaimed "I'm so sorry, look!" And he passed the piece of paper to Jemima.

"But they've included the 250,000 you won in the Grand Slam Running. They can't do that! All the rest of us earned less than the lions. You're the only one to earn more, and that's just because of one running competition. What a mess!"

"Indeed" agreed Cecil as he reached for his calculator. "But they shouldn't have used the mean at all. I'm going to work out the median and see what that is."

"What's the difference?"

"When we talk about the average we normally actually mean the mean." He ignored Jemima's giggle and continued "To get the mean we add up all the individual earnings and then divide by the number of lions or cheetahs. So because of my running win it has made the total of the cheetah earnings very high. The median is the mid range value, so we put the income figures in order of highest to lowest or lowest to highest and then take the middle value. That way one really high figure has no effect. If we have five cheetah's earnings of 200, 300, 350, 400 and 5,000 rand the median will be 350 rand, whereas the mean will be 1,250 rand, which is actually more than 4 of the 5 cheetahs earned!"

"I think I understand," replied Jemima "so with a median a couple of high scores don't have an impact because all the scores aren't added up. So what are the median earnings?"

"The median earning for us cheetahs was 448 rand (put in ascending order the earnings are: 320, 380, 420, 475, 510, 250,000. As there's an even number of scores the median is half way between positions 3 and 4; 420 and 475, with the half rand value rounded up.) For the lions the median was higher at 715. They will be pleased. Now we've got to get the information to the lions without getting eaten!" Cedric passed the piece of paper back to Jemimah and she saw that a new row had been added at the bottom:

Lions		Cheetahs	
SK	1000	J	420
L	670	K	380
MJ	810	S	510
D	520	PT	475
EW	680	C	250,000
FW	750	AZ	320
MEDIAN	715	MEDIAN	448

"That looks a lot better! But what I don't understand is why the mean is used at all if it is so unreliable."

"It's not always unreliable," explained Cedric "often the mean and the median will actually be very close, like they are with the lions. And working out the median in your head or with a calculator can be really difficult; the mean is a much easier calculation! But mean *income is not a good idea as it can be so easily distorted by very high or very low earnings. Other things aren't so susceptible."*

"I've got it. That couldn't happen with age as no-one can be 250,000 years old! Right I'm going to drop this near the lions and then RUN!"

Means, medians and modes are actually all averages, but in everyday language there is a definite tendency for 'average' to be used to mean 'mean'. Confused? Head spinning? I'm not surprised!

What any average attempts to do is summarise data by using one number. Basically that's a task that is too ambitious as it is not really possible to accurately summarise data by using just one number, but that doesn't stop us from trying! And sometimes it is useful. If we know that the average (mean) exam score is 76% we can say that a score of 34% is very low.

Perhaps the root of the problem is that we talk about 'average' in our everyday lives without considering what we actually mean by it. When we talk about an average family, or average person we are normally referring to features that are very common. So a woman of average size immediately brings to mind a woman whose height and weight falls within a certain range. There will be cultural variations within that as average size to an American living in the US will be different to a Japanese person living in Japan. Unfortunately, average does not actually have to refer to a characteristic that reflects 'most people', as the lions and cheetahs example shows.

The **mode** does set out to represent a characteristic possessed by most people, but it can only be used with categorical data (what is meant by categorical data is explained later in the postscript to this chapter). In this example the categories are the kind of pet kept by people living in one town:

Types of pets kept	
Type of pet	n^*
Cats	87
Dogs	46
Rabbits	34
Dragons	98
Snakes	2

*n is the number of pets in each case.

Looking at the list we can immediately see that dragons are the most popular pet; 98 dragons are hopefully being well looked after. We can also see that snakes are the least popular pet as there are only 2 of them. With a list this short where the totals have already been calculated for each category it is very easy just to look to see which is the most frequent. However, imagine if this list contained 10,000 entries with no category totals! That would be very difficult and time consuming. Thankfully many computer programs (including Excel) will calculate the mode. Not all data is suitable for this calculation though. Generally (but not exclusively) a mode is useful when we are interested in the most popular category. Which pet is kept the most frequently? What is the most popular girl's name? Which eye colour is most frequently found? Which alcoholic drink is the most popular? The mode can be calculated to answer those questions and bar charts produced to present the information in a visual way.

The bar chart below refers to our example and shows how many of each type of pet are kept:

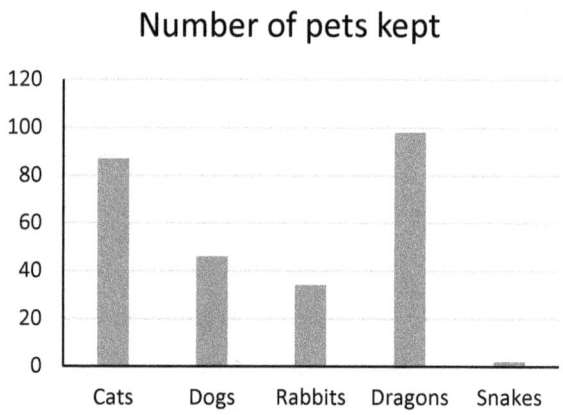

Simply knowing the value of the mode in isolation can be somewhat less than useful. Knowing that dragons are the most frequently kept pet is of limited value. What is of interest is knowing how many other types of pet are kept too. Without a chart or a table giving the totals for other categories we would know nothing about them.

Just for fun let's look at an example of a bad use of the mode:

Candidate no.	Score
1	11.8
2	11.9
3	12.1
4	8.1
5	12.0
6	10.2
7	11.9
8	12.1
9	10.5
10	10.2
11	8.1
12	10.3
13	8.1
14	9.7
15	9.6
16	8.1
17	11.8
18	8.1
19	11.9
20	8.1

For these imaginary exam scores the mode (or modal value) is 8.1. Six candidates scored 8.1, while for other scores only 2 or 3 candidates gained the same mark. But 8.1 is a very poor representation of the data as it is actually the lowest score achieved by the group, all the remaining scores are higher. By contrast the mean (10.23) and the median (10.25) are much more useful. The mode may tell us that the most frequent score is 8.1 but how useful is that information? It is not useful at all. This is not a flaw with the mode itself, it is simply inappropriate to use it in this situation. The reason is that the exam scores are scale data, and the mode cannot be used with scale data. Scale data is data that is obtained from measuring anything that is on a continuous scale. Measuring height and weight are other examples of scale data. Height can be measured using feet and inches or centimetres and meters, in either case the ruler will be a continuous scale.

So what is the best to use? The mean, median or mode? If the data is categorical then we can only use the mode. If the data is scale then either the mean or median can be used; the mean does tend to be used the most frequently, but be wary if the data can have extremes at either end.

Postscript

Scale data is anything that can be measured along a continuous scale, such as height, weight, length, age, income, and test scores. The mean and median are used with scale data, with the median being preferable for income.

Categorical is data that is placed in groups. Just to be confusing there are two types of categorical data; ordinal and nominal. 'Ordinal' data has an 'order' to it. Ordinal data is frequently obtained by putting scale data into groups. Age measured in years is scale, but placing age into categories where group 1 is under 21; group 2 age 21 – 29; group 3 age 30 – 39 etc. is ordinal. The groups have an order as we can see that someone in group 3 is older than someone in group 1. It doesn't matter whether the order goes from less to more or more to less.

By contrast, with nominal data the categories can be interchanged. For example, if eye colour is coded as 1 for blue, 2 for brown and 3 for green there is no logic to choosing those numbers. The coding would work the same if brown was 1, blue 3, and green 2. The important thing to remember is that the mean and median are simply not suitable for categorical data!

However, various computer programs will calculate the mean for categorical data and no warning that the calculation is unsuitable will be given.

One final example (do I hear any sighing?) taking the eye colour example above. For the table on the following page Excel can calculate that the mode is 3, so brown is the most frequent eye colour. It will also calculate that the mean is 2.2 and the median is 2. While it may be useful to know that most people in the group have brown eyes it is of no use to know that mean eye colour is 2.2. For one thing exactly what colour is 2.2? The median colour is green, so we know that if we rank people in order of eye colour the 10.5th person will have green eyes. Great! Completely useless information!

ID (person no.)	Eye colour
1	1
2	3
3	3
4	2
5	1
6	1
7	2
8	2
9	3
10	1
11	3
12	2
13	3
14	2
15	3
16	1
17	3
18	2
19	3
20	3

Where 1 is blue, 2 is green and 3 is brown.

So remember – computer programs have no common sense whatsoever and will calculate whatever you ask them to, however useless that information may be.

CHAPTER FOUR

Correlation

A cautionary revision tale

Juliana was definitely in big sister mode, so she was very cross to see her younger sister Juliette lazing under a tree reading Roar! magazine when she should have been revising.

"Juliette!" she snarled at her sister "Put down that stupid magazine and do some revision! Your Effective Hunting Techniques exam is tomorrow!"

"I know" replied Juliette with a yawn "But I've been talking to other lionesses, and we all agree that you can't learn to hunt by revising for an exam."

"That may be the case, but you have to do the exam tomorrow so you need to revise to make sure you get a good mark."

"Ah! That is the other thing we were talking about! Someone found the results from the exam last year and there was a negative correlation between the amount of time spent revising and the mark in the exam. It was a negative so it means that the more revision a lioness did the worse they did in the exam! As the hours spent revising increased, the scores in the exam actually decreased! Revision really does not help! On the other hand this magazine has some very useful tips on....." Juliette didn't get to finish her sentence as her sister swiped at her with a front paw.

"Ow!! That hurt!"

"Juliette! How many times have I told you that correlation is not causation! Just because there is a correlation between one thing and another it does not mean that one thing happening will result in another thing happening! There could be any number of reasons why the lionesses who did more revision did worse in the exam. You cannot assume it was because they did more revision, however much you may wish that to be the case."

"Well – what else could it possibly be?"

"Don't know, but I am going to find out. So, while I look for the actual data, you do some revision!"

Juliette sighed, but she knew that it was no good arguing with her sister, and she was beginning to feel a little guilty that she wasn't revising. So she reluctantly put the magazine down and turned to her revision notes.

A couple of hours late Juliana returned to find that her sister was asleep with her head on her revision notes.

"Juliette!" she roared "I have the answer."

"The answer to what?" Juliette asked and then quickly remembered as she dodged another swipe from her sister's paw. "My, you are in a bad mood today!"

"I am not in a bad mood, I am just cross with you for not revising, and cross that some lionesses think that correlation means causation simply because they would like it to mean that."

"So – what is the answer then?"

"OK" began Juliana somewhat more calmly "what happened was that last year they made a note of how many hours revision lionesses

did the day immediately prior to the exam. A negative correlation between hours spent revising and exam mark was found, but it's complicated because not all the lionesses were sitting the exam for the first time. Out of the 35 lionesses 15 were re-sitting because they had failed the first time round, so their mark was capped at 40%. This means that for 15 lionesses it was not possible to get a mark higher than 40%, however much revision they did. I looked at the two groups separately to get a better picture of what was happening."
Juliette suspected she was about to have to do a lot more revision and inwardly groaned.

"Separating the two groups showed that for the group sitting the exam for the first time there was no correlation at all between exam mark and time spent revising. Not a positive one or negative one."

"So revision does not result in a higher mark then!" Juliette was beginning to feel optimistic again.

"All it means is that no correlation was found between exam mark and the number of hours spent revising on the day before the exam. How many times have I warned you against last minute cramming? Precisely. We have no idea how many hours the lionesses spent revising in total."

"I don't understand why only the hours spent revising on the day before the exam were recorded. Why not the week before? Or at least 3 days before. Even I don't leave revision til the very last day! Well, not normally anyway."

"I have no idea, maybe it was easier to collect the data that way. Maybe they thought no-one would remember if they asked for more than the day before. Whatever their reason it basically means that not a lot can be interpreted from the results."

Juliette sighed "I suppose I had better keep revising then....."

"Yes indeed. If you're interested, the mean exam score for the first timers was 60%, and the mean number of hours spent revising was 4."

"I've only got two to go then! Great! I still don't think that you can learn how to hunt by studying books."

"And that is a different question altogether" said Juliana as she turned to find a comfy spot in the shade.

Sometimes, we really would like correlation to mean causation, but however convenient it would be for us if it did – it does not. All correlation can tell us is that there is a link between two things. As one goes up the other goes up or as one goes up the other comes down etc.. Unfortunately we cannot state what is causing that link and it could easily be something that we are not even looking at.

Despite the number of times that 'correlation does not equal causation' is emphasised, you will still come across people arguing as if correlation did equal causation. For anything where there is a strong correlation it may well be the case that one thing causes or strongly influences the other, but the correlation itself does not prove that to be the case.

A strong correlation can be a starting point for a new piece of research or analysis which may indeed report that one thing is likely to lead to another. However, the initial correlation cannot do that, it really cannot.

CHAPTER FIVE

Standard Deviation

A tale of two donkeys

Poor Dennis and George were bemoaning their lot when their human told them they would be working in a different place for the coming tourist season.
"Not Santorini!" exclaimed Dennis.
"How many steps to the top are there?" asked George.
"Far too many." was the only possible answer to that question.
Neither donkey relished the prospect of carrying cruise ship passengers from the small jetty where they landed up to the precariously perched village. After muttering about how all cruise ship passengers did all day was eat, George had an idea:
"I know you don't like children Dennis, so why don't I carry all the children? That way your ears will be safe."
"Oh no you don't" replied Dennis, "I'd rather have a child pulling my ears than a 90kg adult telling me how cute I am."
Both donkeys looked at the piece of paper their human had given them. There were two lanes up to the top, one for each donkey. For Lane One the mean passenger weight was 68kg with a standard deviation of 25kg, and for Lane Two the mean passenger weight was 76kg with a standard deviation of 8kg.
"I'll go for Lane One" said George, and to his surprise Dennis agreed.

It was only at the end of the summer that George asked Dennis if he knew anything about standard deviation. He'd noticed that Dennis was not getting the really large people that he was having to carry. "Thankfully I do." replied Dennis. "Basically it's a measure of how much variation there is in the data and how well the mean represents the data. So, although the mean for Lane One was lower than Lane Two the standard deviation was much, much higher. This meant that there was a real possibility of getting people who were quite a bit heavier than 68kg, and lighter too of course. For Lane Two the mean was a much better representation of the data, with much less variability."

George sighed "It makes sense. I had quite a few children, it was their overweight uncles and aunts that were the problem!"

So Dennis gave George another piece of paper which explained how to calculate standard deviation.

Dennis's explanation of standard deviation:

1. Deviation is the difference between an individual measurement and the mean of all the measurements:

Measurement	Mean	Difference
2	0.6	1.4
3	0.6	2.4
-1	0.6	-1.6
-4	0.6	-4.6
3	0.6	2.4

But to find the total amount of deviation we can't just add up all the differences because the +'s and −'s would cancel each other out and give a misleading number. In the example above simply adding up the difference column would give a total deviation of zero, which is simply not helpful.

2. So, to solve that problem we have to square the differences, which will make all the numbers positive. This is much more useful as what we are interested in is how far a measurement is from the mean, not whether it is positive or negative:

Measurement	Mean	Difference	Difference squared
2	0.6	1.4	1.96
3	0.6	2.4	5.76
-1	0.6	-1.6	2.56
-4	0.6	-4.6	21.16
3	0.6	2.4	5.76

The total of the squared differences is now 37.2, which makes a lot more sense. So we could have just compared the squared differences for Lane One and Lane Two and the one with the lowest number would have been the most accurate. The only problem with that is it relies on there being the same number of measurements in each group. If 500 people had used Lane One and only 300 had used Lane Two then we could not compare the sum of the squared differences as we would expect it to be higher for Lane One as more people used that lane.

3. To get round that problem we can work out an average deviation by dividing the sum of the squared differences by the total number of measurements. That would give us 37.2 divided by 5 which is 7.44. (Also known as the variance)

4. Finally, remember that we squared the original differences? So we now need to take the square root, which is 2.73. This is the standard deviation.

George sighed, "That's an awful lot of work just to get one number."

"Don't worry," said Dennis "SPSS (Statistical Package for the Social Sciences) will do it in the click of a mouse."[2]

I can almost hear you thinking "Do I really have to know about this stuff?" Well, it depends.

If the reason you are reading this little book is so that you can understand numbers better, particularly when they are used in the media and by government, then there really is no pressing need to understand this chapter or the next ones. It will be helpful to understand Standard Deviation (SD) though as the figure is often buried somewhere. For example, although a news reports may restrict itself to the mean and percentages, there is often a link that leads to the original research paper, and if the mean has been used there the report will include the standard deviation (SD).

---

[2] Microsoft Excel will also calculate the Standard Deviation, as will other spreadsheet programs

If you are already reading research reports, or know that you are likely to have to in the future, then welcome to Dennis's world! The standard deviation helps to build up a picture of what the data being presented is like. The mistake George made was to think that the lane with the lowest mean weight would be carrying the lightest passengers. In terms of the mean weight that was true, but the mean tells us nothing about the extremes. Remember the cheetahs? One high score can easily distort the mean and taking the standard deviation into consideration is a way of being able to notice when this is happening. If there is a lot of variation in the data, to the extent that the mean is really not a good representation of the data at all, then the standard deviation will help us to recognise this, even if we cannot see the original data.

Imagine we have 2 groups of 50 children who are studying the same course and we are interested in comparing the groups. At the end of the course they take a test; a summary of their scores are presented in the table below:

	N	Minimum	Maximum	Mean	Std. Deviation
Group One	50	10	110	67.26	14.810
Group Two	50	10	110	58.76	31.648
Valid N	50				

For both groups the minimum score is 10 and the maximum is 110. The mean score of Group One is higher than the mean score of Group Two, so it may be tempting to conclude that Group One have performed better. The standard deviation for Group Two is just over twice what it is for Group One, implying that there is much wider variability in the data. The variability in Group Two cannot be explained simply by the lowest and highest scores, as Group One conveniently has the same minimum and maximum scores. So what is happening? Even without looking at the children's actual scores we can deduce that for Group One fewer children are scoring at the extremes while the children in Group Two appear to be 'all over the place'. With this knowledge we may well decide to look at the scores in more detail.

The bar chart below shows the difference between Group One and Group Two. The scores have been grouped so that children scoring between 10 and 19 are grouped together, as are those scoring between 20 and 29; between 30 and 39, 40 and 49 etc..

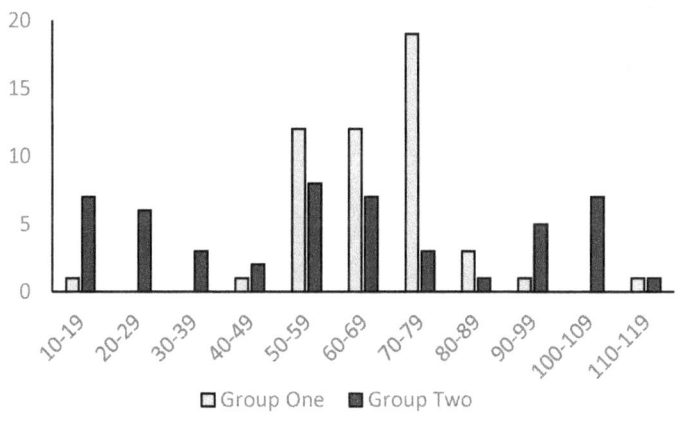

The number of children is shown by the vertical y axis, and the score by the horizontal x axis.

Charts and graphs are very good ways of visually representing differences in the data, and in this case it shows that for Group One most of the children score in the central groupings of 50-59, 60-69 and 70-79. Hardly any children are in the upper and lower groups with some of those groups containing no Group One children at all. No such pattern exists for Group Two, where the scores are spread over the entire range.

There is another use of standard deviation that you may well come across, so we should look very briefly at it here. This use attempts to answer questions such as "When does normal become not normal?"; or "My baby's head circumference is only 50cm, should I be worried?"

Nature is very good at being organised, so the pattern of many, many things is the *'bell shaped curve'*. What this shows is that there are only a few people (or animals or things) at either extreme; most lie in the middle somewhere. You will probably have seen this shape before, if not, here it is:

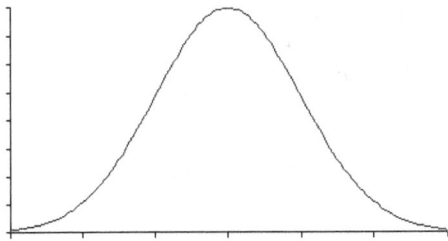

In many fields, people (or animals or things) whose scores lie at the far low end or far high end may be deemed to be 'at risk', or suffering from a particular condition. The standard deviation can be used to decide just how far to the left or right a score has to be before if it of concern. In other words, 'when does normal cease to be normal?'

In 2016 an apparently harmless mosquito bite was linked with birth defects, mainly in Brazil. The birth defect in question was microcephaly; a small head size. But babies do not have uniform head sizes anyway, so we may well wonder how to decide when a baby's head ceases to be just 'small' and the label of 'microcephaly' is applied. Standard deviation can be used for this and here microcephaly is defined as a head circumference that is at least two standard deviations below the mean. That is just one example, there are many, many more.

So, standard deviation cannot be ignored, but how much attention you need to pay to it depends on what you are doing. If you are thinking of collecting and working with your own data, or of working with data that has already been collected, then you definitely will need to understand standard deviation. It can also be useful to know what it is so that when you hear an expert speaking about measurements being 2 standard deviations below or above the mean you know what they are talking about!

CHAPTER SIX

Confidence Intervals

The unConfident Cat

"Are we cats?" Cecil asked Jemimah as she lay down beside him in the shade of a tree.

"Never really thought about it." Jemimah replied "We're cheetahs, that's all I know. Why do you ask?"

"Oh – no particular reason, just curious." Jemimah looked across with a 'don't believe that for a second' kind of expression. Cecil was up to something, she was certain. When she noticed he was reading a magazine article entitled "Never too high to try!" she became even more curious, and then concerned when she saw a photograph of a very high cliff.

"I'm going to google it!" Cecil announced as he reached for his smartphone.

"Well!" he said a few minutes later "I certainly don't like being called a Lesser Cat just because I can't roar! What rubbish!"

"But that still makes us a cat. And I'm sure that we are the quickest of all the cats."

"Yes we are, and it says here that we can accelerate quicker than most of the cars that the humans drive. I've never seen those things moving quickly! They do make good viewing platforms though."

"So are you going to tell me what exactly you have in mind now that you know we are cats?"

"Oh, I'm just going on a trip, nothing major." But Jemimah snatched the magazine before Cecil could stop her and started to read the article. She was horrified. On the opposite page was a photo of a person jumping from the very high cliff, and then another one showing the same person after their parachute had opened. Her eye was caught by a few phrases in the text: 'most extreme of extreme sports'; 'adrenaline junkies'; and 'fatal accidents' were but a few. Cecil was going to try Base Jumping.

"You are not doing it!" Jemimah was very cross, and very worried. "Now I know why you were wondering whether we are cats. You wanted to know whether we have nine lives too! Well I think more than nine lives are needed for that particular sport, you could use them all up in one jump! What on earth are you thinking of!"

"Calm down, I think it looks really exciting, and definitely not something that cheetahs normally do."

"For a very good reason! Most cheetahs have more sense! And what if cats don't have nine lives?" she suddenly thought of a tactic that may at least delay Cecil's trip, and perhaps may stop him going. "Why don't you look at the research? Why don't you get a better idea of how many lives cats have? I think the whole nine lives thing is just a myth."

Reluctantly Cecil agreed and went away to find some answers.

Just when Jemimah was beginning to think that maybe Cecil had changed his mind, he returned with quite a few sheets of paper.

"I've been looking, and there aren't many studies relating to how many lives a cat has. But I found this one which reports the sample

mean to be 8.6 lives and the 95% confidence interval to be between 8.2 and 9.1 lives." He pushed some of the sheets towards Jemimah.
"You really are going to have to explain that." She said as she pushed them back to him.
"Well, the 95% confidence interval is the ....."
"Simple explanation please." interrupted Jemimah.
Cecil ignored her "The 95% confidence interval is basically the range of values that we can be 95% certain will include the true value of the mean of the population we are interested in. We can easily calculate the mean of our sample, the 95% confidence interval calculates a possible range for the mean of the population."
Jemimah waited for him to continue, and when he didn't she said in rather a more surprised tone of voice than she intended,
"Is that it?"
"Yes – calculating it is not straightforward, but the idea is and stats programs do the calculation."
"So – we can only be 95% certain that cats have between 8.2 and 9.1 lives. But that means some cats only have 8 lives!"
"And we can only be 95% certain of that. Normally with something like life and death the 99% confidence interval is used, obviously because that's more certain."
"But still not 100%" interrupted Jemimah, who was beginning to get an idea of where the conversation was heading.
Cecil ignored her again, "so I looked for other studies and found 2 that quoted the 99% confidence interval. In one it was between 8.2 and 9.9 lives, and in the other between 7.9 and 8.9."

Jemimah could not hide her relief. "But that's really good, I mean not good as it shows that cats maybe do not have 9 lives!"

"Correct" *agreed Cecil reluctantly* "I was hoping studies would be reporting confidence intervals where both figures were above 9, then I could be confident that cats do have 9 lives."

"And I think you used at least a couple when the lions were cross with us before."

"I probably did."

"So are you going Base Jumping?"

"I think not."

Confidence Intervals are widely reported by some academic disciplines (such as medical research), and hardly at all by others, while the media restrict themselves to reporting the mean.

First of all an explanation of a couple of words that were used by Cecil: sample mean and population mean. We are always looking at a sample taken from the overall population that we are interested in. In the example above the mean number of lives of a sample of cats would have been calculated (no idea how that could be done!), but what is of interest is how many lives cats in general have. The mean number of lives of the sample of cats is therefore referred to as the 'sample mean', while the number of lives of cats in general is referred to as the 'population mean'. We have to work with a sample because it would be far too time consuming and expensive (and often impossible) to attempt to collect data on everyone we are interested in, and even if we tried we would not succeed. For example, if we want to know more about certain aspects of the population of England we cannot collect data on every single person who lives in England. Even if we had the resources to attempt to do that we would not actually succeed as some people would refuse, some would be on holiday etc.. So it is important to remember that we are always looking at a sample that is taken from the population we are interested in. A sample is chosen to be representative of the population, but it is still a sample. The population itself is an unknown.

This can be really annoying and frustrating. What we are interested in is the group as a whole, whether it's all Year Three school pupils, all people who live in England or everyone who drinks Sprite (other makes of soft drinks are available.) But we cannot obtain data from the entire population; we can only obtain data from a sample of the population. How well the data from this sample represents the entire population is therefore crucial.

It is one of the mysteries of statistics that it is possible to calculate how well something like the mean of the sample represents the mean of the overall population. Do not worry about how that is achieved! People are curious, we want to know the how and why of things, but unless you want to study for a degree in statistics then it is best just to accept that it is possible. You really do not need to know how it is calculated, all you need to know is how well the sample mean represents the mean of the unknown population. If it is a good representation (very narrow confidence interval), then you can look at the results with confidence. If it is a poor representation (large confidence interval that maybe varies considerably between different studies looking at the same topic), then you really cannot say very much at all in relation to the overall population.

By now you could well be wondering how to choose an appropriate sample. That is extremely important and also far from straightforward. It is beyond the scope of this little book though. The topic is widely covered by a range of research books and also explained on a number of university websites.

CHAPTER SEVEN

The Chi-square

and the Pig Whisperer

Betsy was moaning again, it was only a week until the farm open day and she had found a lot to criticise.
"Piglets today have absolutely no idea how to behave! I've just watched them walk down the farm track and not one of them managed to do it without wandering off into the field. They are so naughty! When I was a piglet...."
"You were absolutely perfect and never did anything wrong?" interrupted Elizabeth, who was getting rather tired of these complaints.
"Well no, of course not, I was sometimes a little bit naughty but these piglets are just so naughty, and they have no respect for the farmer, they just ignore him completely!"
"Probably a good thing that he's asked a pig whisperer to help then."
"A pig whisperer? What are they going to do? Whisper directions in the piglets' ears as they walk along? Flibberdejibberdegroat! I've never heard anything so daft!" Betsy was getting very cross and ignored Elizabeth when she tried to interrupt to explain. "What those piglets need is some discipline!"
"Finished?" asked Elizabeth "and then I'll explain."
"OK – shoot."

"Well, a pig whisperer is someone who gains the confidence of pigs by talking in a nonthreatening way, and by building up a rapport. The whisperers use their own body language in a way that we pigs can understand, and they definitely do not yell and hit!"

"Our farmer does not yell or hit either! But the piglets just don't listen to him. How do we know this whisperer person can do any better?"

"Well" replied Elizabeth reaching for an article she had just printed out "coincidentally I have just been reading the results of a study where they compared the effectiveness of a whisperer's training to a normal farmer. And the whisperer did get better results." She pushed the article across to Betsy who looked at it for all of five seconds before complaining that she could not understand it.

"Shall I explain?" asked Elizabeth. In truth, Betsy really wasn't that interested but she thought it would be impolite to say so, so she nodded while at the same time hoping that the explanation wouldn't take too long.

"OK, so they took 100 pigs and the whisperer trained 38 of them and the farmer the rest. Then they checked to see how many pigs could successfully walk along a plank - it was on the ground!" She added hastily on seeing Betsy's expression of alarm. "The task was for the pigs to walk along the plank without leaving it to eat the tasty titbits that were on the ground. The titbits were close, but not close enough for the pigs to reach them without leaving the plank."

"That sounds cruel" interrupted Betsy

"No, it was fine. None of the pigs were deprived of food, and they all got a titbit when they had finished the task."

"So who was the better trainer?"

"The whisperer. A chi-square test showed that the differences were significant."

"A whatta test?" asked Betsy, who was beginning to wish that she had never mentioned the piglets' bad behaviour.

"A chi-square test. A straightforward one is really not that difficult. The easiest way to think about it is to remember that it compares how many of whatever it is we're interested in would be expected to be in each category to how many actually are in each category. Have a look at the tables on page 3."

Betsy turned to page 3 and thought that the tables looked anything but straightforward. "That takes jibberish to a whole new level!" she complained.

"No, you're panicking! Look at it slowly, here I'll explain." Elizabeth moved next to Betsy so she could explain the tables. Here are the tables[3], along with Elizabeth's explanation:

---

[3] These tables are from SPSS. Excel will also calculate the value of a chi-square but you will have to calculate the expected values and enter them into the formula.

whether successfully completed the plank walking task * Who trained the pig Crosstabulation

			Who trained the pig		Total
			whisperer	farmer	
Whether successfully completed the plank walking task	No	Count	16	39	55
		Expected Count	20.9	34.1	55.0
	Yes	Count	22	23	45
		Expected Count	17.1	27.9	45.0
Total		Count	38	62	100
		Expected Count	38.0	62.0	100.0

Table One

"The important thing is not to panic; just look at one thing at a time. This first table (table one above) compares how many pigs were actually in each category with how many pigs we would expect to be in each category if there were no difference in the effectiveness of the farmer's and the whisperer's training. The top row looks at the pigs who did not successfully complete the task; the 'no' row. The next part down looks at the pigs who did complete it; the 'yes' row, and the final part is the total of all the pigs regardless of whether they completed the task successfully or not. They are in the 'total' row at the bottom.

So if you look at the pigs who did not complete the task 16 were trained by the whisperer and 39 by the farmer, but remember that overall 38 pigs were trained by the whisperer and 62 by the farmer, so we would expect to have more pigs trained by the farmer in every category. The next row down is therefore very important as it tells us how many pigs we would expect to find in that category if there were no difference between the effectiveness of the 2 trainers. If there were no difference we would expect to see 20.9 pigs trained by the whisperer not being able to complete the task. This is because overall 38% of pigs were trained by the whisperer and 55 pigs did not complete the task. With no difference in the effectiveness of the training we would expect to see 38% of these 55 pigs trained by the whisperer, which is 20.9 pigs (don't worry about portions of a pig!). But, there were only 16 who did not complete the task, so the whisperer did better than we would expect. Similarly we would expect to see 34.1 pigs trained by the farmer unable to complete to the task (62% of 55), but there were 39, so the farmer did worse than we expected.

If we go down to the 'yes' rows, more pigs completed the task than expected if they were trained by the whisperer, and fewer pigs than expected if they were trained by the farmer. So we can see that the farmer had fewer successful pigs than expected while the whisperer had more. What the chi-square does is test to see whether those differences are significant.

Sometimes it can be nice to be able to state the percentage in each category as that makes comparisons easier. But we have to be really careful as not all the percentages are useful! In this example SPSS will calculate the percentages for us, all we have to do is click on a box to tell it to do so. But - the box we click on is very important, we have to be careful!"

whether successfully completed the plank walking task * Who trained the pig Crosstabulation

			Who trained the pig		Total
			whisperer	farmer	
whether successfully completed the plank walking task	No	Count	16	39	55
		Expected Count	20.9	34.1	55.0
		% within Who trained the pig	42.1%	62.9%	55.0%
	Yes	Count	22	23	45
		Expected Count	17.1	27.9	45.0
		% within Who trained the pig	57.9%	37.1%	45.0%
Total		Count	38	62	100
		Expected Count	38.0	62.0	100.0
		% within Who trained the pig	100.0%	100.0%	100.0%

Table Two

"Table Two gives us a useful percentage as it shows the percentage of successful and unsuccessful pigs according to who trained them. This is the column percentage so we now need to look vertically at the columns. For the whisperer we can see that 42.1% were in the 'no' category 16 out of 38 pigs), while 57.9% were in the 'yes' (22 out of 38). The final row just tells us that the whisperer trained 38 pigs.

For the farmer we can see that 62.9% were in the 'no' category (39 out of 62), and only 37.1% in the 'yes' (23 out of 62). The columns separate out the whisperer and the farmer, so it does not matter at all that the farmer trained more pigs than the whisperer.

However, the row percentage is not useful, which is shown in Table Three"

whether successfully completed the plank walking task * Who trained the pig Crosstabulation

			Who trained the pig		Total
			whisperer	farmer	
whether successfully completed the plank walking task	No	Count	16	39	55
		Expected Count	20.9	34.1	55.0
		% within whether successfully completed the plank walking task	29.1%	70.9%	100.0%
	Yes	Count	22	23	45
		Expected Count	17.1	27.9	45.0
		% within whether successfully completed the plank walking task	48.9%	51.1%	100.0%
Total		Count	38	62	100
		Expected Count	38.0	62.0	100.0
		% within whether successfully completed the plank walking task	38.0%	62.0%	100.0%

Table Three

"The problem with the row percentage is that because the farmer trained more pigs there are likely to be more pigs in each category, and there are. The 'total' row tells us that overall 62.0% of the pigs were trained by the farmer and 38.0% by the whisperer. So that 70.9% of the pigs that were unsuccessful were trained by the farmer and only 29.1% by the whisperer is of limited value. For the pigs that did complete the task 51.1% were trained by the farmer and 48.9%

by the whisperer. Without looking at the entire table simply quoting this row percentage would give a misleading picture, so should not be done! This is another example of a computer program having no common sense. Remember it will perform a calculation if it is possible to perform it, regardless of how appropriate or useful that calculation is!"

Elizabeth was pleased with her explanation, but when she turned round Betsy was fast asleep.

A chi square result can be reported in many different ways. Sometimes you will see a table, sometimes you will just see "differences were significant (p<.05)". Sometimes you will see the value of the chi-square (4.118 in this case), the number of degrees of freedom (df here it's 1 as there are two trainers (you don't have to worry about that at the moment!)), along with the significance level (.042). However the results are reported, in this example we can say that the pigs trained by the whisperer performed significantly better than the pigs trained by the farmer.

Significance

So, what is significance? First a light bulb joke:

"How many statisticians does it take to change a light bulb?"

"One, but the change has to be significant."

At the moment that joke is probably just not funny (and it may still be not funny once you've read the explanation below, but at least you will hopefully understand it).

What a test for significance sets out to do is establish the point at which we can state with a reasonable degree of certainty that the result we have obtained is not simply a result of chance, that something really is 'going on'. For example, if I claim that I can predict whether a coin will land heads or tails and a coin is thrown and my prediction is correct that in itself will not provide evidence of my claim; I could simply have been lucky and guessed the correct answer. Even if I can predict two coins in a row that could still just me being lucky. As more coins are added to the prediction at some point people would begin to think that there was something to my claim, that I really could predict how a coin will land and it was unlikely that I had predicted the result simply by guessing. Note that little world 'unlikely'. Sometimes people can be amazingly lucky; falling out of a plane, landing on a haystack or something similarly soft and surviving does happen, but the majority of people who fall out of a plane without a parachute will not survive.

So we need to look at the probability of the result being obtained by chance, which in turn tells us how certain we can be that there really is something going on. Before computers and stats programs extremely clever people had to work this out by hand, and it took a very long time. Now we just do a few mouse clicks and the tables appear in seconds! We do need to understand the information in the tables though.

One significance level that is frequently used is the 95% level. At this level we can be 95% certain that the result is genuine and it has not been obtained by chance. But, do remember that being 95% certain still means that there is a 5% chance that the result is not genuine, that it is a result of guesswork or other chance events.

When you see significance levels reported you will not see 95% quoted as the figure. This is because the probability value is used when reporting significance, not the percentage. However, one can be calculated from the other. Probability can only lie between 1 and 0, where 1 is absolutely definite that something will happen (100%), and 0 absolutely no chance at all that it will happen (0%). For the coin throwing example, if one coin is thrown a person has a 1 in 2 chance of guessing correctly. The coin will either land heads or tails and the person will make one guess (either heads or tails). So they are making one prediction for two possible events. One divided by two is .5, which in turn is 50%. (To turn probability into a percentage multiply by 100.)

It is these probability values (p values) that the computer programs calculate. A 5% possibility that the result is not genuine, that it is the result of chance is a probability of .05 (5 divided by 100). If the p value is less than .05 we can say that there is less than a 5% chance that our result has been obtained by chance, there really is something going on; the result is therefore significant.

As we will see in the next couple of pages other significant p values can be used as well, but for the moment it is only important to understand the concept of significance.

Understanding statistical significance is not made any easier by the way we use the word significant in our everyday speech. We talk about significant events, or a person making a significant contribution etc.. In that context the word implies importance. When used in statistics, it may be important in the above sense, or it may not be, it all depends on what is being measured.

Statistically testing for significance may result in finding something that is important or interesting, but it may also result in finding something that is unimportant or boring and predictable. A test for significance is purely a test, the interest lies in what we apply the test to. For example, over a year we could measure the mean temperature at the equator and compare it with the mean temperature at the South Pole. Undoubtedly we would find that the temperature at the equator is significantly higher than the temperature at the South Pole. It would give a statistically significant result, but also a totally boring result.

That is an extreme example, but when faced with pages and pages of tables stats programs such as SPSS produce it can be tempting to look for anything where the magic significance level has been met. Do not do that – ever! Looking for significance should be driven by questions that you are looking for answers to.

Formulate the question first and then look for significance; do not look for significance and then find a suitable question!

Similarly, just as a significant result does not mean that something is important or interesting, a non-significant result does not mean that something is not important or boring. If there was no significant difference in the health of those living in the poorest areas of the UK compared to those living in better off areas that would be very interesting. Unfortunately it is not the case. So do remember that significance simply means that we have measured something and applied a statistical test to the result.

To continue we need the help of some cups of tea. You may have come across someone who claims to be able to tell whether the milk has been put in the cup before the tea was poured, or added after the tea was poured. If you haven't then humour me and use your imagination. If we pour a cup of tea and ask this person whether the milk has been added first or not we will not be impressed if they give the correct answer as we know that they have a good chance of guessing the correct answer. With the only options being 'milk first' or 'tea first' they have a 1 in 2 (or 50%) chance of guessing the correct answer. If we gave them more cups of tea and they kept correctly identifying whether the milk or tea had been added to the cup first then at some stage we would decide that they really could tell the difference, that they were not simply guessing.

There are a number of versions of a story concerning Fisher (a very important statistician) and cups of tea. The details vary, but the gist of the story is that he was at a garden party in the 1920's when he met a lady who claimed she could tell whether the milk or tea had been added to the cup first. Apparently if the hot tea is added first then it scalds the china and affects the taste. He decided to put her ability to the test and discovered that yes, she could tell the difference.

Fisher formulated a number of important experimental designs which form the basis of many of today's studies. His refinement of the 'cups of tea' experiment was crucial in deciding where a widely accepted level of significance is. Imagine 6 cups of tea, three of which have had the milk added first and three the tea. There are 20 different orders that these cups can be presented in. Just so you can count them, in the diagram below the arrows indicate where the milk has been added first:

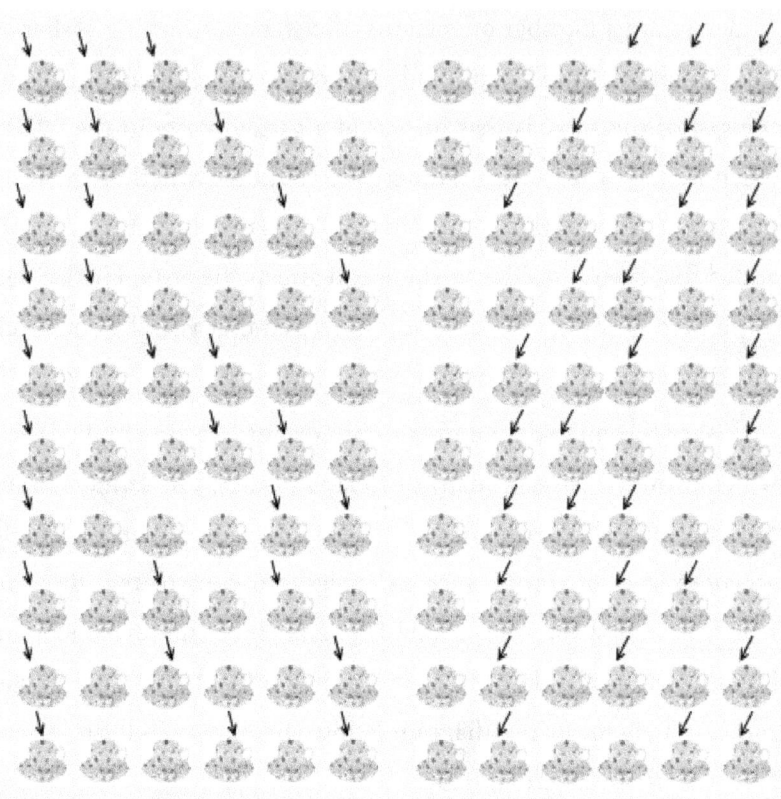

With 20 possible 'layouts' for the cups of tea there was only a one in 20 chance of guessing correctly (1 divided by 20 gives a probability of .05, or 5%). With a 5% chance of guessing the correct answer if someone correctly identifies whether the tea or milk has been added first then we can be 95% certain that the result is genuine and not the result of chance. (If you're struggling a bit we return to this with lions and straws in Chapter Eight).

However, we are now in the early 21st century, rather than the early 20th century so it is not surprising that many people disagree with Fisher and his cups of tea. If you are interested then there is no shortage of reading material available, but for the moment we will restrict ourselves to the idea of the 'magic' 5%. This 5% is a probability of .05, and it is this probability figure that stats programs use in their tables. You may be thinking that the cut off point is somewhat arbitrary, and to some extent it is! In Fisher's time people had to use tables that were published by very clever people. Fisher produced tables giving these critical values (or cut off points) for probabilities .05, .02 and .01. Over time, the values of .05 and .01 became commonly used. Fisher himself acknowledged that the strict use of a cut off point was not sound practice, but that did not stop people enthusiastically publishing results where the significance level was quoted simply as <.05. A study which found a significance of even slightly over .05 could not make the magic statement: "….result was found to be significant (p<.05)" and was often left unpublished and ignored, even though the result could have been important and interesting.

This consigning to the rubbish bin is just one of the arguments against the strict use of significance testing. We will not consider the others here, just remember that stating that a result is significant (or not significant) is just the result of applying a statistical test, it is up to you to interpret that result.

CHAPTER EIGHT

The *t* test

"The plot has officially been lost, by you." said Juliana as she looked down at her younger sister Juliette.

"No, not at all!" complained Juliette. "It's not just me that thinks so, lots of other lionesses think the same, even the ones in a different pride."

Juliana looked very concerned "You have been speaking with lions from another pride? That is very foolish! What were you thinking of?"

"Oh it was fine! The male was fast asleep as usual. Anyway, they agreed with me that the antelope on the north side of the river are much tastier than the antelope on the south side. So I'm going to do a comparison and publish the results in Big Cat Diary To-day! Don't you think that's a brilliant idea?"

Juliana knew that Juliette wasn't really asking her opinion so she merely grunted a reply and moved to follow the shade of her tree. "And how are you going to compare antelope?" she asked.

"Well I'm going to catch 2 antelope from each of the herds and give them a tastiness mark out of 10. That will show which herd is tastier!"

Juliana thought about replying and then decided that it was far too hot to get into an argument with her younger sister, so she merely sighed, muttered "Good Luck", then turned around and went to sleep.

A few days later Juliette found her sister asleep under the same tree. "I was right!" she said excitedly, "the antelope to the north of the river are tastier than the ones to the south! Will you help me write the article for Big Cat Diary To-day?
Juliana reluctantly sat up and asked her sister how she came to that conclusion.
"Well" explained Juliette "the first antelope from the south wasn't too bad, the first one from the north only tasted slightly better actually. But then the second antelope from the south did not taste very good at all whereas the one from the north was absolutely delicious! So overall the ones from the north won in the tasty stakes!"
"Oh Juliette. Did you pay any attention to Maths lessons at school? Do you remember studying t-tests? Do you remember an independent samples t-test?"
"Of course I paid attention!" Juliette said defensively, even though the truth was that she hardly ever turned up, never mind paid attention. "I don't remember those classes though. Why are they important?"
"You hinted at the reason yourself. You said that there wasn't much difference between the first two antelopes. So - how do you know that you didn't, purely by chance, choose the worst tasting southern antelope and the best tasting northern antelope as the second pair of antelopes?"
"So what would a t-test do?"

"If we conducted a proper statistical test it would tell us how likely it was that the results we obtained could have been obtained by chance. It would tell us whether we could be confident that there really was a difference in taste or whether it was likely to all be a result of chance."

"Statistics cannot do that! Can't eat antelope!"

"No, but statistics can help us to know whether we may have obtained results by chance. I can explain if you want."

"No, it's OK" replied Juliette as she settled down in the shade of the same tree. "I'm really not interested, I'll stick to eating the antelope. You can do the tests if you want."

So what Juliette couldn't be bothered with is actually very important. If we are comparing two groups and want to be able to say that one group scores significantly higher (or is larger, smaller, younger etc.) than the other group we need to be confident that we haven't, by chance, chosen group members who are not really representative of the group. The way this is done is really very complicated and guaranteed to result in brain ache, but the good news is that you do not need to know how it is done, only that it is done!

Straws and Boxes

Let's imagine 2 boxes of straws, with around 200 straws in each box. We are interested to know whether there is a difference in the length of the straws in each box. We can't see inside:

Box One   Box Two

The first straw that we pull out of Box One looks like this:

While the first straw we pull out of Box Two is:

We repeat this until we have chosen 5 straws from each box:

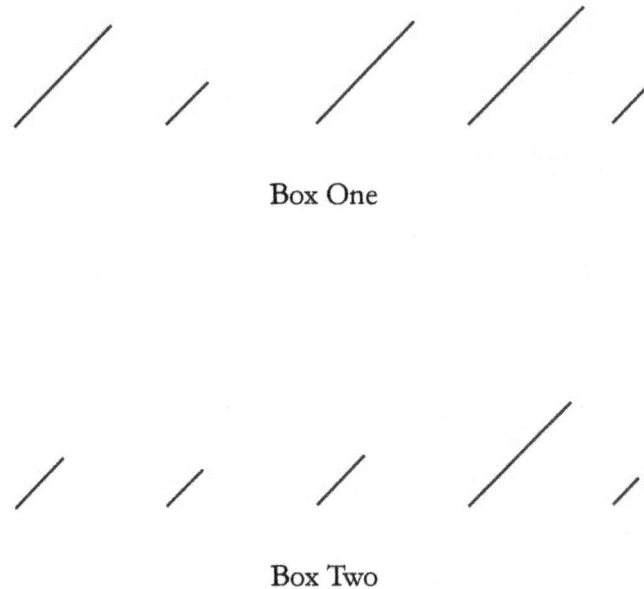

Box One

Box Two

OK – so we are now probably convinced that the straws in Box One are longer than the straws in Box Two. But are they really? Or, could we, purely by chance have pulled out mainly long straws from Box One and mainly short straws from Box Two? We had previously decided that we were going to sample 20 straws from each box and so continue until 20 straws have been selected and measured. And no, there is no diagram showing pictures of the 20 straws, life really is too short to do that.

After 5 straws we probably would have confidently stated that the straws in Box One were longer than the straws in Box Two. But was it purely chance that meant that longer straws were selected? It is precisely this situation that an independent samples t test is suitable for. Various computer programs will run the test so it is not necessary to know how it is calculated. What is important is to understand the basic principles behind the test, and also when it can and cannot be used. This example uses straws and boxes but the technique can be used in any situation where we are interested in comparing the same measure across two different groups. The height of children in two different classes or the total rainfall in two different cities etc.. It can be used wherever the assumptions described below are met:

First of all, the two samples must be truly independent. That may sound a bit obvious, but real life situations can easily mess this one up. If you are comparing two different classes of children then the children must always have been in the same different classes. If a child switched classes then the samples are not truly independent.

The second thing relates to the size of the groups. Some very quick background history. The t test was developed in the very early 1900's by a statistician working for the Guinness brewery in Dublin. When he published his statistics work the brewery wouldn't let him use his real name (Gosset), so he published it simply referring to himself as 'Student'. The test was developed for a practical situation where all data was collected by hand and analysis was conducted using ink and many sheets of paper; sample sizes were not large. Now, thanks to computer progams and the ready availability of large data sets we do not have such restrictions. If you are looking at an analysis of a government survey there will probably be thousands of respondents. This is the situation where a t test **cannot** be used. There are other tests that can be (and outside the scope of this little book – you may utter a sigh of relief), but a t test simply cannot be used. This is not a 'fault' with the test, it was simply not designed to be used with large samples and if it used it will find even small differences to be significant.

At this stage there is no need to try to understand why that is the case. It is easier to accept that it just is and if you come across an article that is making claims based on a t test conducted on large samples, then look carefully, and be prepared to dismiss their 'findings'. Just because a t test may show that differences were statistically significant, it does not mean that the differences actually were important. With a thousand people in each group even small differences will become significant. Practically speaking, they are not, a t test should not have been used.

But back to our boxes. Are the straws of similar length or not? First of all, a summary of the 20 straws from each box that make up our sample (without pictures!):

	Box	n	Mean	Std. Deviation	Std. Error Mean
Length of straws in cms	1	20	4.30	1.895	.424
	2	20	5.70	1.593	.356

Taking each column in turn, the first tells us we are measuring the length of the straws, the second which of the two boxes they are in, and the third that we sampled 20 straws from each box. In the 'Mean' column we can see that despite the first 5 straws we pulled out from the boxes suggesting that Box One contained longer straws, when the complete sample of 20 straws were measured the mean length of the sample from Box One is actually shorter than the mean length of Box Two's sample. Standard Deviation (Std. Deviation) was explained in an earlier chapter (Dennis the Devious Donkey, Chapter Five) but what is Standard Error of the Mean?

OK – if we took lots of different samples from our population of interest (we could put those 20 straws back and select another twenty straws and measure them) then we would expect to get a slightly different mean for each of the samples. In an ideal world these means would be very similar, reflecting the fact that because the different samples are taken from the same population their differences are not going to be that great. In the same way that we worked out the Standard Deviation of the sample, so we can work out the Standard Deviation of these different sample means. If the differences between the samples were only slight then this figure would be small. However, if we are taking smallish samples from a large population where there is a lot of variance then we may expect quite a lot of difference between the mean of one sample and the mean of another. This would result in a much larger Standard Error of the Mean (SE).

The Standard Error of the Mean is therefore a way of seeing how well our sample mean represents the population from which the sample was drawn. In a perfect world (ever seen that?) it would be zero or close to zero as different samples from the same population would have very similar means. In reality this just isn't going to happen, but for our straws it is small, so we can be happy that our sample is a good reflection of the population of straws from which it was drawn. (And this is another occasion where it is best not to attempt to wonder how this is calculated!)

So – now for the independent samples *t* test:

	t test for Equality of Means				
	Sig (2 tailed)	Mean Difference	Std. Error Difference	95% Confidence Lower	95% Confidence Upper
Length of straws in cms	.016	-1.400	.553	-2.520	-.280

There is now only one row because it is the difference between the two boxes that is being summarised; the test is assessing whether the two means are the same or different. Taking each column in turn:

The first reminds us that we are looking at the length of straws. This may seem obvious but when your head is spinning it is surprisingly easy to look at the wrong table! So we know we are actually looking at the correct table – Phew!

The second is "Sig. (2-tailed)", and the figure is .016. This tells us that the difference between the two means is significant as it is less than .05. The '2-tailed' is because we have not predicted which direction the difference is going to lie in; we have not predicted whether Box One or Box Two will have the longer straws.

The third simply tells us what the difference between the two means is: 4.30 – 5.70 is – 1.40. If the boxes had been labelled so that Box Two became Box One then it would have the higher mean, resulting in a positive difference.

The Standard Error of the Difference tells us how well the difference of our sample (20 straws from each box) represents the difference of the unknown population of straws. (Remember – do not stress about this! It is one of those seemingly impossible things that stats packages can do!)

The final two columns state the upper and lower limits of the 95% confidence interval. Remember the unConfident Cat? (Chapter 6) This is the interval that we can be 95% certain contains the true difference between the means of the unknown populations. Basically, the wider the interval is, the less confident we can be. So, in the context of our straws we can be 95% certain that the true difference between the means lies between -2.520 and -0.280. They are both negative, so we can be 95% certain that the mean length of the straws in Box Two is always longer than that of the straws in Box One.

So, we now know that the straws in Box One are significantly shorter than the straws in Box Two. Do I hear you wondering whether it was worth the effort?

Assumptions

If you know that you are never going to conduct your own *t* test, and the previous section caused brain ache then do not worry about the next part! If you are likely to want to conduct your own *t* test then read on. However, this section will not be sufficient in itself to enable you to do that.

If you are going to conduct your own independent samples *t* test then you will need to make sure that the data is suitable. We have already looked at the need for the samples to be truly independent, and to be of an appropriate size. There are also other assumptions that have to be met.

- A *t* test relies on the data having a normal distribution. A normal distribution is one that is found very frequently in nature, and was mentioned briefly in the chapter about standard deviation (Chapter Five). We see examples of the normal distribution all around us; very few people are very small and very few people are very tall, most people lie somewhere in the middle. Plotting a graph gives what is imaginatively called 'The Bell Shaped Curve'. (See example in Chapter Five).

- The variance of the groups must be similar. Remember Dennis the Devious Donkey (Chapter Five)? If one group has scores that vary very little, while the other group has scores that are turning variance into an extreme sport, then we cannot say that the variances are similar. Statistical programs will run tests for 'Homogeneity of Variance' to check this.
- The data must be at least interval data. Interval data is a continuous scale where the differences between any two points on the scale represent the same amount of difference in what is being measured. For example, responses to questions such as 'On a scale of 1 to 10 (where 10 is the highest) how would you rate your satisfaction with the comfort of your bed?' are at interval level. The comfort is not given an actual score, but the difference between 1 and 2 is the same as between 9 and 10. Or, the data can be
- Scale data, where the data is continuous and a measure of something physical (height, weight etc.) or mental (anxiety score) are absolutely fine.

Although that list may seem daunting, it isn't really. It's worth noting that independent samples t tests are usually conducted using scale data. It's also worth mentioning that there are other kinds of t tests. For example, a paired sample t test looks at changes over time. A measurement is taken at one point in time and then repeated later to assess any changes.

These tests are very useful and we can learn a lot about data from them, but a final note of caution is needed. Remember that they are just the same as any other statistical test, they can tell us many things about our data, and help us to build an accurate picture, but it is always our responsibility to interpret the results. Don't do the equivalent of following a SatNav down a dead end road.

And finally….

You made it to the end of the book! Congratulations! Despite any reservations you may have had at the beginning, you managed to get here. You have now hopefully lost your fear of numbers, even if you still do not consider them to be your best friend.

Do not worry if you found the final chapters somewhat daunting. The final t test chapter in particular is introducing more difficult concepts, so it's OK to struggle a bit (or a lot). And do remember that it really is not necessary to understand statistical tests for everyday understanding of numbers; when the media and government mislead us with numbers they frequently do so with percentages and means. Whether this is deliberate in order to support whatever point they wish to make, or just laziness, we may never know.

Hopefully now when you see a statement that 'people who eat unripe bananas are 15% more likely to….. (get tummy ache? Turn yellow? Have difficulty peeling them?)' your instant reaction will be to think "15% of what? How many people who eat ordinary bananas are likely to experience the same thing?"

And if you see a statement that the mean annual income of under 25's is £40,000 you will wonder how many professional premier league footballers (or similar high earning occupations) were in their sample. Mean income really should come with a health warning, a few high salaries can distort the mean considerably, so median income is much preferable.

If you are now confident with both of the above then well done, that in itself is an achievement. Don't dwell on what you still don't understand, spend some time thinking about the new things that you now do understand.

And if this little book was for you a starting point, if you are a student and you know that your course content will lead you to more numbers, then good luck, you can do it.

And remember

Numbers

are

Nice!

www.ingramcontent.com/pod-product-compliance
Lightning Source LLC
Chambersburg PA
CBHW071314040426
42444CB00009B/2017